WHY WE LIVE WHERE WE LIVE

by Lisa Oram

PEARSON
Scott
Foresman

Editorial Offices: Glenview, Illinois • Parsippany, New Jersey • New York, New York

Sales Offices: Needham, Massachusetts • Duluth, Georgia • Glenview, Illinois
Coppell, Texas • Sacramento, California • Mesa, Arizona

Where People Live

If you live near an ocean, you might enjoy playing in the water. Someone you know might earn money by fishing. You may have seen a hurricane. If you live near an ocean, your daily life might be connected to the water.

Wherever you live, your daily life is connected to that environment. People live in many different places on Earth, and these **locations** affect the **cultures** of the people who live there.

People adapt, or adjust to, their surroundings. For example, people who live in cold climates cannot change the weather, but they can learn how to keep warm.

A community forms where people can live safely and can get the supplies they need. A **community** is a place where people live, work, and have fun together.

Water

When you look at a map or a globe, you will see lots of blue areas that represent water. Water includes the rivers, lakes, streams, and oceans that cover almost three-fourths of Earth's surface.

Water is necessary for humans to live, so people often live where water is plentiful. Lakes and rivers provide water for drinking, cooking, and washing. Fishing provides food for many people around the world.

Many people enjoy living near water because of its natural beauty. They can also take part in water sports, such as surfing, swimming, and canoeing.

Living near water can sometimes be dangerous. Severe storms with heavy rains can cause floods that might damage homes and buildings. People who live near water must also know how to work and play safely.

Oceans are huge bodies of salt water that separate large areas of land. There are four oceans on Earth. They are the Atlantic Ocean, the Pacific Ocean, the Arctic Ocean, and the Indian Ocean.

The United States is bordered by the Atlantic Ocean and the Pacific Ocean. Many large cities are located on ocean coasts because of the shipping and fishing industries. These businesses need many workers, so many people are able to find jobs.

Communities are often located near rivers, another source of water. Rivers are large streams of fresh water that flow into another body of water.

Before there were many roads, rivers were used for **transportation**. After railroads were built, **populations** could grow in towns far away from rivers.

Farming communities can usually be found near rivers. This is because the rivers are a good water source for growing crops.

Lakes are bodies of water surrounded on all sides by land. Most lakes are freshwater, but some are salt water. Thousands of years ago, large sheets of ice called glaciers moved slowly across the earth. The glaciers carved holes that filled with water from rain or melting ice to make lakes.

Some people live on islands, or pieces of land that are surrounded on all sides by water. Islands can be found in lakes, rivers, or oceans.

Life in island communities is affected by how far the islands are from the mainland. Some islands are connected to the mainland by bridges. People can drive to and from the island easily.

Some islands have no bridges and can only be reached by plane or boat. In that case, people on the island must plan carefully if they depend on supplies from other places. When there is bad weather, it can be difficult to get supplies.

Deserts

People have lived in deserts since ancient times. Desert populations are usually very small. Deserts are dry places that receive less than ten inches of rain per year.

Weather in the desert is extreme. The days are very hot and the nights are very cold. There are sandstorms with high winds in deserts. People who live in the desert must have shelter and clothing that protect them from the harsh conditions.

In some places, people who live in the desert move around to find water supplies. Their homes are tents that are light and easy to pack and carry. In some modern desert homes, there may be air conditioning.

Desert clothing must be light to keep a person's body cool. It is also important to wear a hat and sunscreen in the desert.

Some deserts are always cold. The continent Antarctica is a desert with lots of ice and snow. It hardly ever rains or snows there.

Moving Mountains

Mountains are tall, natural landforms that rise into peaks, or tops. The air at the peaks of mountains is colder than the air below, so many mountaintops are covered with snow all the time. As the temperature changes, snow melts and runs down the mountain into the streams and rivers. People drink from these freshwater sources.

Mountain areas can be a challenge for people. For early explorers getting over or around mountains was very difficult. Today, many countries have roads and tunnels that make travel in and through mountains much easier.

Mountain land is often too rocky and steep for growing food or raising cows. There are often small communities in mountain valleys. There are also cities on the edges of some mountain regions.

Sharing the Land

All communities share their surroundings with plants and animals. There are flowers that grow in the mountains that grow nowhere else. Cactuses grow in the desert because they can survive with little water. Each environment affects the types of plants and animals that live there.

Every community is special. All communities have cultures with customs and traditions related to the environment around them. Transportation, food, and clothes all connect people to where they live.

Glossary

community a place where people live, work, and have fun together

culture the arts, beliefs, behavior, and ideas of a group of people

location where something can be found

population the number of people in an area

transportation a way of carrying things or people from place to place